21st
Century
Skills Library

REAL WORLD MATH: GEOGRAPHY
OCEANS

BY ANN HEINRICHS

Published in the United States of America by
Cherry Lake Publishing, Ann Arbor, Michigan
www.cherrylakepublishing.com

Content Adviser
Andrew Dombard, Associate Professor, Department of Earth and Environmental
Sciences, University of Illinois at Chicago
Math Adviser: Tonya Walker, MA, Boston University

Credits
Photos: Cover and page 1, ©Chris Anderson, used under license from Shutterstock,
Inc.; page 4, ©Blaine Harrington III/Alamy; page 7, ©Yiannos1/Dreamstime.com;
page 8, ©iStockphoto.com/oversnap; page 10, ©Durden Images, used under license
from Shutterstock, Inc.; page 13, ©Ingvar Tjostheim, used under license from
Shutterstock, Inc.; page 14, ©iStockphoto.com/stevegeer; page 16, ©Elisei Shafer,
used under license from Shutterstock, Inc; page 19, ©Ovidiu Iordachi, used under
license from Shutterstock, Inc.; page 20, ©iStockphoto.com/Photomick; page 24,
©iStockphoto.com/rbouwman; page 27, ©Exploretimor/Dreamstime.com

Library of Congress Cataloging-in-Publication Data
Heinrichs, Ann.
 Oceans / by Ann Heinrichs.
    p. cm.—(Real world math: geography)
 Includes index.
 ISBN-13: 978-1-60279-496-2
 ISBN-10: 1-60279-496-0
 1. Oceanography—Juvenile literature. 2. Ocean—Juvenile literature. I. Title.
II. Series.
 GC21.5.H45 2010
 551.46—dc22   2008052362

Cherry Lake Publishing would like to acknowledge
the work of The Partnership for 21st Century Skills.
Please visit *www.21stcenturyskills.org* for more information.

TABLE OF CONTENTS

CHAPTER ONE
**DIVIDING THE WORLD
OCEAN**. 4

CHAPTER TWO
**DEPTH, SEA LEVEL, AND
PRESSURE**. 10

CHAPTER THREE
**DO THE MATH: SALTY, COLD,
AND DARK**. 14

CHAPTER FOUR
**DO THE MATH: CURRENTS
AND TIDES**. 20

CHAPTER FIVE
**HEALTHY OCEANS FOR A
BETTER LIFE**. 24

REAL WORLD MATH CHALLENGE
ANSWERS 29

GLOSSARY 30

FOR MORE INFORMATION 31

INDEX. 32

ABOUT THE AUTHOR. 32

CHAPTER ONE
DIVIDING THE WORLD OCEAN

Tomasi scrunches his toes in the white sand on his way down the beach. He wades into the shallow waters of the Pacific Ocean with his bamboo pole to spear fish. Meanwhile, Jacob rides his dogsled down to the ice-covered coast.

Hawaii is a series of islands in the Pacific Ocean. Beachfront resorts are popular vacation spots.

There he watches a seal and its pup floating on a chunk of ice in the Arctic Ocean. Both boys live on the edge of an ocean. As different as their lifestyles are, they share the same body of water.

Ocean waters cover 71 percent of Earth's surface. This water is really one big ocean with land sticking out above its surface. We call this big ocean the World Ocean. We divide the World Ocean into several ocean areas according to their locations and common features.

LIFE & CAREER SKILLS

Over time, people have counted anywhere from three to seven oceans. Today, the International Hydrographic Organization (IHO) makes the call. The IHO is responsible for describing and measuring oceans. The IHO once recognized four oceans—the Atlantic, Pacific, Indian, and Arctic. In 2000, it added a fifth ocean, called the Southern Ocean, to its list. However, some geographers consider the Southern Ocean an extension of other larger oceans. Take a look at a world map. If you were making the rules, how many oceans would you count? Why?

Who can say where one ocean ends and another begins? Throughout history, people developed ways of distinguishing one ocean from another. Usually, large bodies of land lie between them. Today, geographers identify five major oceans: the Pacific, Atlantic, Indian, Southern, and Arctic oceans.

The largest ocean of all is the Pacific Ocean. This huge expanse of water stretches from the continents of Asia and Australia on the west to North and South America on the east. It covers about 60,000,000 square miles (155,399,287 square kilometers). That's about 30 percent of Earth's entire surface.

Next in size is the Atlantic Ocean. It's bordered on the west by North and South America and on the east by Europe and Africa. Shaped like an hourglass, the Atlantic Ocean is narrower than the Pacific Ocean and less than half as big. The Atlantic Ocean covers about 29,630,000 square miles (76,741,348 sq km).

REAL WORLD MATH CHALLENGE

The United States covers about 3,794,000 square miles. **How many times would the United States fit into the Pacific Ocean?**

(Turn to page 29 for the answer)

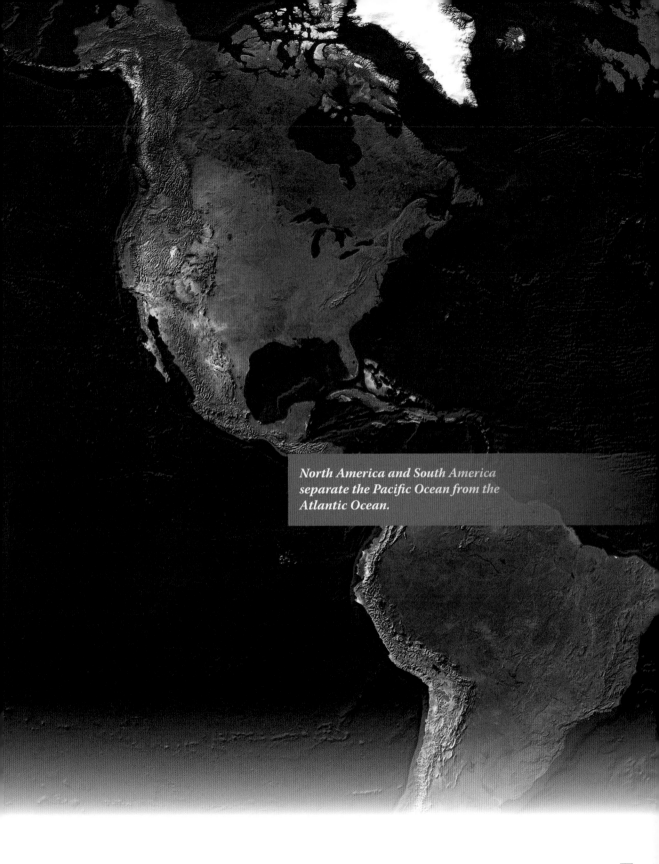

North America and South America separate the Pacific Ocean from the Atlantic Ocean.

The Indian Ocean stretches between Africa and Australia, reaching northward to southern Asia. Its area is about 26,463,000 square miles (68,538,855 sq km). The Southern Ocean encircles the continent of Antarctica, which lies atop the South Pole. This ocean covers about 7,846,000 square miles (20,321,047 sq km). The smallest ocean is the Arctic Ocean, with an area of 5,426,000 square miles (14,053,275 sq km). It covers the region around the North Pole. Most of its water is frozen as a thick, drifting pack of ice.

Large chunks of ice float in the Arctic Ocean.
The ice makes sailing dangerous for ships.

One way of locating the oceans is by **hemisphere**. The Northern Hemisphere is north of the equator—an imaginary line running east to west around Earth's center. South of the equator is the Southern Hemisphere. The Arctic Ocean is entirely within the Northern Hemisphere, and the Southern Ocean lies in the Southern Hemisphere. The equator cuts through the middle of the Atlantic and Pacific oceans. It divides them into the North Atlantic, South Atlantic, North Pacific, and South Pacific oceans. As for the Indian Ocean, it's mostly in the Southern Hemisphere and partly in the Northern Hemisphere.

Smaller branches of the oceans are called seas. Often seas are partly enclosed by land. For example, the Mediterranean Sea is almost completely surrounded by Europe, Asia, and Africa. Its waters join the Atlantic Ocean through the narrow Strait of Gibraltar.

The word *sea* is often used to describe the oceans themselves. It also shows up in terms related to oceans such as seawater, sea level, and seafloor. Let's look at the math involved in some of these features.

CHAPTER TWO
DEPTH, SEA LEVEL, AND PRESSURE

Pinocchio, the fictional wooden boy, sank down to the bottom of the sea. A submarine went down there, too, in the science fiction movie *Voyage to the Bottom of the Sea*. But where is the bottom of the sea? And just how far down is it?

Because the ocean is so deep, shipwrecks can be hard to find. They are also dangerous to explore.

Pinocchio would have sunk about 4,920 feet (1,500 meters). That's the average depth of the Mediterranean Sea. It surrounds Italy, where Pinocchio lived. He was lucky he didn't sink in the Pacific Ocean, the deepest ocean on Earth. Its bottom is an average of 14,040 feet (4,280 m) below the surface. That's more than 2.5 miles (4 km)! The Atlantic Ocean is the second deepest, at 11,810 feet (3,600 m). The shallowest ocean is the Arctic Ocean. Its average depth is about 4,300 feet (1,311 m).

LEARNING & INNOVATION SKILLS

The bottom of the Mariana Trench is often called the Challenger Deep. It's named for the British ship HMS *Challenger*, which first measured the trench's depth in 1875. To do this, the crew lowered a rope with a heavy weight on the end. When the rope stopped descending, they knew the weight had reached bottom. By counting markers placed along the rope, they could calculate the distance. Can you think of any problems with measuring the ocean's depth this way?

REAL WORLD MATH CHALLENGE

Jeremiah wants to be a deep-sea explorer. He hopes to explore the bottom of the Mariana Trench. Down there, the pressure is about 16,000 PSI. Jeremiah wants to get an idea of how heavy that would feel. His pet pig weighs ¼ of a ton. (Hint: 1 ton = 2,000 pounds.) **How many pigs per square inch would equal the pressure in the Mariana Trench?**

(Turn to page 29 for the answer)

Deep valleys called trenches plunge far below the sea-floor. The deepest trench is the Mariana Trench, in the Pacific Ocean. That's where the submarine in *Voyage to the Bottom of the Sea* went. This trench reaches a depth of 36,198 feet (11,033 m). That's the lowest point on the planet. If the sea has a bottom, the Mariana Trench is it!

Oceans are used to measure land heights, too. A mountain's height is given in terms of feet (or meters) above sea level. Sea level is the average level of the ocean's surface. It doesn't matter if a mountain is sitting on land that's already high. The distance of its peak above sea level is the height that counts.

Anyone exploring the ocean knows the math of water pressure. At sea level, air has a pressure of 14.7 pounds per

A remote-controlled submarine is lowered into the water. Remote-controlled submarines allow scientists to explore the deep sea without putting themselves in danger.

square inch, or PSI (1 kilogram per centimeter). But water is heavier than air, so it exerts more pressure. For every 33 feet (10 m) you descend underwater, the pressure increases by another 14.7 PSI. This puts dangerous pressure on air spaces in the body, such as lungs, ear canals, and sinuses. Deep-sea vessels must have heavy walls. Otherwise, the water pressure would crush them. Ocean exploration can be dangerous, but divers and **oceanographers** keep safe by doing the math!

CHAPTER THREE

DO THE MATH: SALTY, COLD, AND DARK

"Water, water, everywhere, nor any drop to drink." These lines are from a poem about sailors lost at sea.

A pile of salt sits next to salt ponds. At salt farms, ocean water evaporates from shallow pools leaving salt behind.

Their drinking water had run out. However, as all sailors know, they shouldn't drink seawater, even if they're dying of thirst. Why is this?

Seawater is saline, or salty. It's full of minerals called salts, which wash from Earth's crust. If someone drinks seawater, water in the body bonds with the salts and gets eliminated in urine and sweat. This removes more water from the body than the person has taken in.

Oceanographers measure **salinity** by weighing parts of salt per 1,000 parts of water. On average, seawater has a salinity of 35. That is, every 1,000 tons of water contains 35 tons of salt. That's the same as 3.5 percent salt. Most of that salt is sodium chloride—the same type of salt you sprinkle on your food.

REAL WORLD MATH CHALLENGE

Nicholas wants to mix up a batch of seawater to see what it tastes like. He learns that 1 cup of water weighs 236 grams, and 1 teaspoon of table salt weighs 6 grams. **How many teaspoons of salt should he mix into an 8-cup pan of water to make it as salty as seawater?** (Remember: seawater is 3.5% salt.)

(Turn to page 29 for the answer)

Seawater is cold, too. If you're sweltering on the beach, you know you can jump into the water to cool off. The ocean's surface layer, nearest to the Sun, is the warmest layer. The average temperature there is 63.5 degrees Fahrenheit (17.5 degrees Celsius). Surface temperatures can range from 93°F (34°C) in the Indian Ocean's Red Sea to 28.4°F (−2°C) in the Southern Ocean's Weddell Sea.

Temperatures plunge rapidly in the **thermocline**, the layer beneath the surface. In the deep layer, below the

Life is plentiful near the surface of the ocean.

thermocline, it's literally freezing. Much of the deep layer is 32 to 37.5°F (0 to 3°C). Why doesn't ocean water freeze? Because it's so salty. Salt water has a lower freezing point than freshwater. Freshwater freezes at 32°F (0°C). But seawater with a salinity of 35 freezes at about 28.4°F (−2°C).

Sunlight can reach down into the oceans about 655 feet (200 m). This upper region is called the **photic zone**. Here trillions of microscopic plants called phytoplankton carry on **photosynthesis**, using sunlight to produce nutrients. Phytoplankton are the basis of all life in the oceans. About 90 percent of all sea life lives in this zone, including sharks, whales, jellyfish, sea turtles, and lobsters.

REAL WORLD MATH CHALLENGE

Humpback whales feed in cold waters and migrate to warmer waters to breed. Some humpbacks begin their migration in the Southern Ocean, where the water temperature is 30°F. They swim about 5,200 miles (8,369 km) north into the North Pacific Ocean, where the water is 82°F. **On average, how many degrees (F) does the water temperature rise for every 1,000 miles they swim?**

(Turn to page 29 for the answer)

LEARNING & INNOVATION SKILLS

Sonar uses sound to find objects under the water and to measure ocean depth. During World War II, the navy used sonar to hunt for enemy submarines. While searching for these subs, sailors noticed something odd. Each night, their sonar showed the seafloor moving up into the photic zone. By dawn, the seafloor would go back down into the twilight zone again. Scientists soon learned that this moving "seafloor" was really large groups of fish. What does the photic zone have that these fish might need? Why might they visit the photic zone at night, when everything is dark?

Below this level is the so-called twilight zone, down to about 3,280 feet (1,000 m). There you'll meet dragonfish with bulging eyes and long, sharp teeth. Farther down, to about 13,120 feet (4,000 m), are gulper eels with gigantic jaws, and vampire squids.

These jellyfish light up in the deep parts of the ocean. Many animals living in the deep ocean can do this.

CHAPTER FOUR
DO THE MATH: CURRENTS AND TIDES

E leven-year-old Wayne Broderick of Maine wrote a note and put it in a bottle. Then a local fisherman tossed it into the Atlantic Ocean for him. Two years later, Wayne

Sailors find currents useful. Following a current helps them travel much faster.

received a letter from a girl who lives in the Azores Islands, more than 2,500 miles (4,023 km) away! Thanks to ocean currents, Wayne has a new pen pal.

Currents flow like giant rivers in the ocean, moving seawater around the planet. They are caused by factors such as winds and Earth's rotation. Currents swirl in large, circular loops called **gyres**. Gyres in the Northern Hemisphere rotate in a clockwise direction. Those in the Southern Hemisphere spin counterclockwise.

REAL WORLD MATH CHALLENGE

On January 1, 2007, Greta threw a bottle into the Atlantic Ocean off the coast of North Carolina. Someone in Mauritius, an island in the Indian Ocean, found the bottle on March 21, 2010. It had traveled about 9,400 miles (15,128 km). **What's the average number of miles the bottle traveled each day?** (Hint: Remember that 2008 is a leap year.)

(Turn to page 29 for the answer)

Two of the strongest currents are the Kuroshio Current and the Gulf Stream. The Kuroshio Current flows through the North Pacific Ocean, off the coast of Japan. The Gulf Stream travels up the United States' east coast, then drifts northeastward across the North Atlantic Ocean. These currents can move as fast as 5 miles (8 km) an hour. That's more than 100 miles (161 km) a day!

Ocean voyagers must know the direction and speed of the currents around them. Following a compass, they might head for a spot directly to the west. But the current could carry them southwest instead. They would never reach their destination!

21ST CENTURY CONTENT

The tidal range is the difference between the water level at high tide and at low tide. Canada's Bay of Fundy gets the most extreme tidal range on Earth—48 feet (14.6 m). Canadian engineers built a power station there. It harnesses the energy of the moving tidewaters to generate electricity. What other ocean movements could be used to produce electric power?

Tides are another type of ocean movement. Tides are the regular rise and fall of the ocean's surface. They are mostly caused by the **gravitational** pull of the Moon. The Moon pulls on the water nearest to it, making a bulge in the ocean.

Waters on the opposite side of Earth bulge at the same time. These two bulges create high tides, where water rises high up onto the seashore. In between the bulges are low tides, where coastal waters recede and expose more land.

Cycles of high and low tides occur within a time period of 24 hours and 50 minutes. That's a lunar day—the time it takes the Earth to rotate so that the moon is in the same part of the sky again. Most seacoasts get two high tides and two low tides every lunar day. Some places get just one high and low tide a day, or a mixture of high and low tides.

If you're tying up a boat on the seashore, you'd better know the tide schedule. Either check a tide table, or do the math in your head. Otherwise, your boat might be stuck on a dry beach at low tide. At high tide, your boat could be stranded out in the sea!

REAL WORLD MATH CHALLENGE

Ivan went out on his fishing boat all day. When he got back at 8:15 P.M., he anchored his boat on the shore. He returned at 6:00 the next morning to find his boat way out in the ocean. Ivan's coastal village gets two tide cycles a day. **How long does he have to wait till he can get back in his boat again?**

(Turn to page 29 for the answer)

CHAPTER FIVE
HEALTHY OCEANS FOR A BETTER LIFE

O ceans have a lot to do with our lives up here on dry land. Take food, for instance. Fish and other

Fish markets are a good place to find fresh fish. Markets are usually near an ocean, where the fish are caught.

seafood are important sources of protein. We need protein to keep our muscles, blood, and other body tissues healthy. The oceans supply us with about 90 million tons of seafood every year!

Oceans clean the air we breathe, too. Burning **fossil fuels** such as oil and coal releases tons of carbon dioxide (CO_2) into the atmosphere. The CO_2 pollutes the air, causes health problems, and traps heat close to Earth. But the ocean's phytoplankton consume CO_2 during photosynthesis. Scientists estimate that the oceans absorb 30 to 50 percent of the CO_2 from fossil fuels.

21ST CENTURY CONTENT

The world's seafood catch leveled off in 1989. Some scientists predict that the ocean's seafood population will almost completely disappear within 50 years. This raises concerns about food supply as the world's human population rises. Many countries practice aquaculture, or raising seafood on "fish farms." What other things might people do to help increase the ocean's seafood population?

Oceans also affect our climate. When water evaporates from the oceans, it forms rain clouds. The rain nourishes our grasses, trees, and food crops. Ocean temperatures and wind patterns cause violent storms, too. These storms are called hurricanes in the Atlantic Ocean and typhoons in the Pacific Ocean. Earthquakes on the seafloor also cause tsunamis—gigantic waves that cause mass destruction on land.

Unfortunately, humans are damaging the oceans. One example is the Great Pacific Garbage Patch. This massive collection of garbage floats in the North Pacific Ocean. It may cover as many as 5 million square miles (13 million sq km)—an area larger than the entire United States! Most of the garbage is plastic, such as plastic bags and bottles. Fishing lines, nets, cans, toys, flip-flops, and tires are in there, too. Fish and other ocean wildlife get tangled up in the mess. They eat the garbage, and it comes back to humans in seafood. Waste dumping and oil spills pollute the oceans even more.

Scientists use math to study the oceans. They measure **pollutants** in ocean water and in the bodies of fish. Other scientists use math to study ocean temperatures, currents, and wind speeds. Some study deep-sea life, and there's plenty to study. About 300 million to 500 million species of plants and animals live in the ocean!

Corals sometimes build new homes on old human garbage.

REAL WORLD MATH CHALLENGE

About 100 million tons of plastic are manufactured every year. Scientists estimate that 10 percent of all plastic ends up in the ocean. Seventy percent of that plastic eventually sinks deep down below the surface. **How many pounds of plastic sink deep into the ocean every year?** (Hint: 1 ton = 2,000 pounds.)

(Turn to page 29 for the answer)

We can get involved in these issues, too. Using math, we can learn how the oceans behave and how they support life. Knowing the math facts, we can form wise opinions and maybe even choose an ocean-based career. After all, the future of the oceans is in our hands.

REAL WORLD MATH CHALLENGE ANSWERS

Chapter One

Page 6

The U.S. could fit into the Pacific 15 times.

60,000,000 sq mi ÷ 3,794,000 sq mi = 15.814 = 15

Chapter Two

Page 12

The pressure equals 32 pigs per sq. in.

0.25 x 2,000 lbs = 500 lbs
16,000 PSI ÷ 500 lbs = 32 pigs per square inch

Chapter Three

Page 15

Nicholas needs 11 teaspoons of salt.

3.5% = 0.035

236 g x 0.035 = 8.26 g of salt for each cup of water

8.26 g x 8 cups = 66.08 g of salt for 8 cups of water

66.08 g ÷ 6 g = 11.01 = 11 tsps

Page 17

The temperature rises 10°F for every 1,000 miles the whales swim.

82°F – 30°F = 52°F

5,200 mi ÷ 1,000 mi = 5.2 mi

52 ÷ 5.2 = 10°F

Chapter Four

Page 21

The bottle traveled an average of 8 miles per day.

3 years from 2007 to 2010.

3 years x 365 days = 1,095 days

2008 is a leap year, with an extra day in February.

1,095 + 1 = 1,096 days

80 days from Jan. 1 to March 21.

January has 31 days, February has 28 days, and March has 21 days.

31 + 28 + 21 = 80 days

80 + 1,096 = 1,176 days

9,400 mi ÷ 1,176 days = 7.9 = 8 mi per day

Page 23

Ivan has to wait 2 hrs and 40 min.

24 hours, 50 minutes ÷ 2 = 12 hours, 25 minutes

8:15 P.M. + 12 hours, 25 minutes = 8:40 A.M.

Ivan came back at 6 A.M., so he will have to wait 2 hours and 40 minutes to get his boat back.

8:40 – 6:00 = 2:40

Chapter Five

Page 28

Every year, 14 billion pounds of plastic sink deep into the ocean.

10% = 0.10

100 million tons x 0.1 = 10 million tons

70% = 0.70

10 million tons x 0.7 = 7 million tons

7 million tons x 2,000 pounds = 14,000 million pounds

14,000 million pounds = 14,000,000,000 = 14 billion pounds

GLOSSARY

fossil fuels (FOSS-uhl FYOOLZ) substances, such as oil, coal, and natural gas, that are formed from the remains of plants and animals

gravitational (grav-ih-TAY-shuhn-uhl) relating to gravity, the force that pulls two objects toward each other

gyres (JIRES) circular loop patterns in which ocean currents move

hemisphere (HEM-uhss-fihr) half of a ball-shaped object such as Earth

oceanographers (oh-shuh-NOG-ruh-furz) scientists who study the oceans

photic zone (FOH-tik ZOHN) the upper layer of the ocean where sunlight can reach

photosynthesis (for-toh-SIN-thuh-siss) the process by which plants convert sunlight into chemical energy

pollutants (puh-LOO-tunts) harmful substances in the air and water

salinity (suh-LIN-uh-tee) saltiness

thermocline (THUR-muh-kline) the ocean layer below the surface, where temperatures decline rapidly

FOR MORE INFORMATION

BOOKS

Burns, Loree Griffin. *Tracking Trash: Flotsam, Jetsam, and the Science of Ocean Motion.* New York: Houghton Mifflin, 2007.

Ingram, Scott, and Joellyn M. Ausanka (editors). *Oceans.* Milwaukee: Gareth Stevens, 2004.

Nye, Bill, and John Dykes (illustrator). *Bill Nye the Science Guy's Big Blue Ocean.* New York: Hyperion, 2003.

WEB SITES

Oceans Alive! Looking at the Sea
www.mos.org/oceans/planet/index.html
Fascinating facts about the oceans and their geographic features

Office of Naval Research: Oceanography
www.onr.navy.mil/focus/ocean/
A survey of ocean regions, waters, movements, and animal habitats

INDEX

Arctic Ocean, 5, 6, 8, 9, 11
Atlantic Ocean, 5, 6, 9, 11, 20, 21, 26

Bay of Fundy, 22

carbon dioxide (CO_2), 25
Challenger Deep, 11
climate, 26
currents, 21–22

depth, 11, 12, 17–18

Great Pacific Garbage Patch, 26
Gulf Stream, 21
gyres, 21

hurricanes, 26

Indian Ocean, 5, 6, 8, 9, 16, 21

Kuroshio Current, 21

Mariana Trench, 11, 12
marine life, 17, 18, 24–25, 26
Mediterranean Sea, 9, 11

oceanographers, 13, 15

Pacific Ocean, 4, 5, 6, 9, 11, 12, 17, 21, 26
photic zone, 17, 18
photosynthesis, 17, 25
phytoplankton, 17, 25
pollution, 25, 26, 28

Red Sea, 16

salinity, 15, 17
seafloor, 9, 12, 18
sea level, 9, 12–13

sea water, 9, 15, 16, 21
sonar, 18
South Atlantic Ocean, 9
Southern Ocean, 5, 6, 8, 9, 16, 17
South Pacific Ocean, 9
Strait of Gibraltar, 9

temperatures, 16–17, 26
thermocline, 16
tides, 22–23
trenches, 11, 12
tsunamis, 26
twilight zone, 18
typhoons, 26

water pressure, 12–13
Weddell Sea, 16
World Ocean, 5

ABOUT THE AUTHOR

Ann Heinrichs's sea adventures include voyages in the Atlantic Ocean, the Mediterranean Sea, the Irish Sea, the Red Sea, and the South China Sea. Ann has written more than 200 books. Originally from Fort Smith, Arkansas, she now lives in Chicago, Illinois. She enjoys kayaking, bicycling, and traveling to faraway places.